Gilded Verse

Anthology — whispers of the heart woven into words

Banasmita Das

BookLeaf Publishing

India | USA | UK

Made with ❤ on the BookLeaf Publishing Platform
www.bookleafpub.in
www.bookleafpub.com

Dedication

To my *grandparents*, whose morals and values linger in the breeze, a quiet reminder of roots that run deep

To my *parents*, the pillars of my world, whose love transcends time and space

To *Sushmita* and *Nipu*, my elder sister and brother-in-law, my guiding stars whose support is both my light and my refuge

Preface

In the delicate pauses between utterances and the fleeting silences between heartbeats, poetry emerges like a shadow at twilight, elusive yet ever-present. This collection, born of such moments, is a reflection of the myriad emotions that weave through our lives—the silent joys, the tender sorrows, the quiet revelations that shape the contours of our being. It is a journey not only of personal reflection but of shared humanity, where the echoes of individual experiences intertwine with the universal truths that transcend time and place.

These poems are not mere words on a page; they are fragments of a larger conversation—one that touches the unspoken, gives voice to the invisible and illuminates the quiet wisdom hidden in the spaces between thoughts. They are as much a record of my own soul's wanderings as they are an invitation for you, dear reader, to wander alongside me.

Each verse is a mirror, each line a thread, inviting you to find your own reflection within the tapestry of these words. In this shared space, may we both discover the art of listening—to the heart, to the silence and to the language that transcends us all.

Acknowledgements

This anthology is not simply a collection of verses, but a living testament to the hearts and the lives that have touched mine, in ways both subtle and profound and whose presence, whether brief or enduring, has left an indelible mark on my soul. Each line and word, carries within it the echo of your influence—an offering of gratitude for the love, the challenges, the triumphs and the silence that have shaped me into who I am.

My family and friends, whose laughter, wisdom and presence have provided both solace and inspiration— your support has been the silent pulse beneath every verse. I owe a deep debt of gratitude to my mentors, whose teachings have shaped the contours of my craft, offering insights that have carved paths through the murk of uncertainty.

To every reader who has found meaning in these words —whether in fleeting moments or in quiet contemplation —your engagement breathes life into what would otherwise remain mere ink and paper.

Finally, to poetry itself, for being both a mirror and a lantern, a way to understand and a way to transcend. This book exists because of the support, the challenges and the love that continue to shape my every line.

Echoes of a lost warmth

Foggy wintry and *blur*
it seems too far is summer
A distant echo, like a forgotten hummer

The frost upon my window paint tales untold
Of sunlit days and evenings bold
Is January a painter with cold strokes and sighs
Or merely the whisper of my heart and a time that flies

A blanket of memories cozy and warm
But I feel the chill—like an unsettled storm
I wonder if it's something I've misplaced
A fragment of joy that I once embraced

Yet through the haze, my heart does remember
That fleeting warmth—was it last September?

Foggy wintry and *blur*, yes, I am missing summer
But perhaps it is not lost, just waiting to recover

Through Dew and Dusk

Dewdrops and misty mornings
November hues and my musings

Your silhouette in the dusk of my heart
The vehemence of love and art

Winter and snowfall at the doorstep
Waiting in forbearance
To embrace a season
imbued with poignance

I stand and stare at the desolate sky
The moon is crescent
and the stars are shy

I hark back about you
and your Midas touch
It's *November*
and I am missing you
a little too much

Symphony of Silence

In *hushed* tones, I confine my soul
A quietude that makes others whole
They fret and fuss, with worried face
At my reserved words and silent space

But little do they know, the din within
A maelstrom of thoughts, a turmoil to spin
The noise that I harbor, a cacophony of pain
A symphony of secrets, I dare not proclaim

So let me hold my peace and keep my thoughts at bay
For in the stillness, I find a way
To navigate the chaos and calm the raging sea
And in the silence, discover serenity

Heaven Orenda

The *celebration* of the heaven
Throwing confetti all around
With every falling flake
A unique spark meets the ground

A fluffy white blanket
And a picturesque glance
Like angels from up above
Fluttering in grace and elegance

I woke up and opened my eyes
But the dream still alive in my heart
Oh! I love snowfall
Nature is truly a *prodigy* in art

Soul beyond skin

Sometimes I wonder, in the quiet of the night
If ever the world, in its blind hasty flight
Shall look past the surface, the shimmer, the gleam

And see the true beauty that lies within
Not the fleeting reflection that passes the eye
But the warmth in your heart, the love you deny

Sometimes I wonder, when all masks have been cast
If anyone notices the soul that will forever last
The one that was shaped by celestial hands
Crafted with care from the finest of strands

It is not the face that the Gods sought to mold
But the soul within-*ageless and bold*

Oh, how they forged a beauty that transcends the skin
A radiance that grows, from the heart deep within
So rare is this treasure, this grace to behold
A *beautiful soul*, more precious than gold

Sometimes I wonder, if anyone will see
The treasure you carry so humbly and free
For it's not in the eyes or the smile or the face
But in the soul's warmth, that holds endless grace

Born from Broken

And after the *tears* had dried, her heart did stir
A quiet strength arose from where once was blur
Through deepest shadows, where no light had shown
A *pure* dawn pierced, and claimed her as its own

Her *voice* once trembling, now rang strong and clear
A melody though weary, without fear
No longer bound by what was held too tight
She *stood, unshaken,* bathed in softest light

Bruised, beautiful and bare, she dared to stand
Stripped of comfort, with truth clasped in her hand
Each scar a testament to battles fought
Yet in her veins, new roots of courage caught

For in the breaking, *blooms* the tender grace
A garden born from every empty space
Where once was silence, now the wild winds sing
Of the woman who rose, and spread her wings

Blooming where the brokenness was once sown
She found the strength to stand, to be alone
But not in solitude, for in her core
She carries light that shone through every door

And now she blossoms, fierce, free and true
A masterpiece from above, that was crafted to rule
To live, to love, to rise from past despair
And *bloom, unafraid,* in the *strength* of being bare

Her Joy her Grace

Grace—true grace begins
When she walks with courage, free from whims
When her *jhumkas* and *bindis* gleam
Each piece of her a part of some dream

Grace is when she wears her style with pride
Carries her attitude, nothing to hide
Her *payal* tinkle, a soft sweet sound
That soothes my heart and makes the world spin around

Grace is when she dons a *Mekhela Sador*
Her beauty, which the world adores
With every fold, every flutter of cloth
She holds the essence of the earth, the sky—both

Grace is when she teases with playful air
Whispers her mischief into the silence, rare
Her voice, a soft murmur in my ear
A tender jest that draws me near

Grace is when her smile,
Transforms my sorrow, makes it worthwhile
With gentle hands and a heart so kind
She turns my despair into peace of mind

It feels as though each grace she holds
Is tailor-made, in silver and gold
And grace is when she, in every part
Finds happiness in her own heart

For *Grace* is not just beauty worn
It is in the joy she's always born
Grace, true grace, is not a fleeting glance
It is in the way she makes life dance

Shine through your Roots

Some *run* from the soil that once gave them life
Chasing a world that sharpens like a knife
They trade their roots for a fleeting face
To fit in the crowd, to find some grace

But life, it strikes with an unseen hand
And brings them back to the shifting sand
When the world turns cold and hearts grow tired
They return to the warmth of what inspired

Now authenticity wears the crown
Originality, the talk of the town
The world is waking, at last it seems
To the power of truth and the strength of dreams

So, wear your *roots*, let your values shine
Help make the world a better place, divine
Celebrate what makes you truly you
And let the world, in your light, renew

Her Presence: A melody

I love your playful ways, so sweet
Your beauty makes my *heart* skip a beat
To lose to you in every smile
And win you back, makes it all worthwhile

When you turn with a teasing glance
Or love me with your quiet trance
Your every step, your graceful sway
Is a song I wish to hear each day

I cherish your mischief, wild and free
To bear your tantrums, lovingly

The *tinkle* in your eyes, the *chime* of your bangles
The music of your steps, like distant angels
Each sound you make, a sweet refrain
That soothes my soul and breaks my pain

For in your arms, I find my bliss
A *queen* adorned in love's soft kiss

When Silence speaks

The *silence* that falls when wishes come true
The ones you feared, the ones you knew
A prayer, once whispered, now answered clear
And silence tells you the cost of the fear

The silence that lingers when hearts don't match
When kindness fades and truth we can't catch
The weight of knowing not all are the same
And silence speaks of the unspoken shame

The silence that follows after giving all
And still, you find no rise, but a fall
Empty hands, yet a heart still full of grace
The quiet speaks of the void in this place

The *silence* that comes after words we regret
Once said in haste, we can't forget
The quiet tells us what time can't undo
And silence reminds us of things we knew

Rebirth in thirties

In my *twenties*, I searched with eager eyes
A quest for the self beneath the endless skies
I stumbled, I questioned, I lost and I found
As I chased the reflections within my mind

But the thirties arrive, like a dawn's first light
Ceremonial, a pause before taking flight
A moment to breathe, to step back and see
What truly aligns with the soul you wish to be

Now, as a woman in this vibrant new phase
I have come to cherish the quietest gaze
The truth I once sought now lives in my bones
In the work I create, in the love I have outgrown

A blank slate, a gift, a chance to unfold
To carve out the life that's bright and bold
No longer bound by what others expect
I claim the life that my heart will protect

Luxury of calm

We grumble at the cycle, round and round
Morning's bell, the chores, the familiar sound
The same routine, each day a mirror clear
A life unchanged and yet so dear

But in this rhythm, peace is quietly sewn
No stormy waves, no seeds of fear are grown
How blessed we are, with steady hands and light
To wake and sleep in calm, night after night

For in the simple, there's joy to find
The comfort of a life, soft and kind
To wake, to work and rest again
Is a luxury, where others see only strain

So cherish the days that seem all the same
In their quiet, there's no shame
For the peace of home, steady and bright
Is the greatest gift, a silent delight

Magic in grey

For every person who thinks you're "*too quiet*"
There's one who sees your silence as bright
An amazing listener, with a heart so clear
Their words find comfort when you're near

For every person who thinks you're "*too clingy*"
There's one who loves your care so true
The way you open your heart so wide
And show your love with nothing to hide

For every person who thinks you're "*too sensitive*"
There's one who sees strength in your grace
In every feeling, raw and pure
They find the beauty, the soul's allure

For every person who thinks you're "*too confident*"
There's one who finds your self-respect divine
An inspiration, bold and true
Your inner strength, a light that shines through

Strength in Faith

Strength comes from within
A fire that no storm can dim
Your *happiness*, a light inside
No need to look, it's where you reside

The Divine walks with those who trust
In their own hearts, both pure and just
In faith, the soul finds its true way
Guided by *power*, day by day

Believe in the *Supreme*, beyond the skies
The force that in every being lies
In silence, in love, in every prayer
The *Divine* is with you, always there

Camaraderie of soul

I call in the voices of kindness and grace
Those who speak truth with an open face
I call in the hearts that embrace the light
And those who bring warmth to the darkest night

I call in the courage to stand in my own
The strength to be gentle, yet deeply grown
I call in the ones who are ready to explore
The vastness within and what's yet in store

I call in the bonds that are rooted in trust
Where love is a language and words are just dust
I call in the souls who dance in the rain
Together we rise, through joy and through pain

I call in the wisdom to always be true
To honour my journey and honour yours too
In every breath, in every stride
I call in all that the universe provides

Whispers between pages

I miss the voice who shared my mind
In endless talks of books we would find
To some, just pages, black and white
To me, they are calm in restless night

Books are my refuge, soft and deep
A world where thoughts can gently sleep
In every word, I find my way
They keep me sane, come night or day

I miss the voice that shared the thrill
Of finding meaning, at my will
Books, my meditation, calm and deep
They keep me sane, they help me sleep

For though their meaning shifts and bends
In every word, a message sends
I miss the one who understood
That books, to me, are more than good

Tales from my perch

A *bird* on my perch, wings brushed by the sky
From distant lands, it soared so high
It tells me *tales* in the soft evening glow
Of places it's been, of faces below

The day is its own, with skies stretched wide
But the evening is mine, as we both collide
Through its eyes, I wander far
Seeing the world, near and afar

Some faces *gleam* with joy, others wear *despair*
Yet no one stops to gaze, or even care
In this quiet moment, we both understand
The *silence of souls* in a vast, empty land

No Spells, Just Love

She is not a magician, no spell she weaves
Yet when I return, wearied by the day's grieves
I find in her gaze, a tender balm
A peace that quiets the storm, so calm

Her face, like the sun's first tender light
Unravels my burdens, restores the night
No incantations, no sorcery grand
Yet in her presence, the world is unmanned

How do you do it, this magic untold
With a smile that turns all to gold?
Maa, with a glance you set me free
A haven of warmth, where I long to be

Rise and Strive

I work to meet the bills, it's true
But deeper still, there's much to do
To learn, to grow, to stretch my mind
And leave the weight of doubt behind

I seek a refuge, calm and near
A place where I can shed my fear
To challenge fate and carve my way
And rise anew with each new day

I work to touch the world, to see
A legacy take shape in me
For joy in effort, peace in stride
For truth that cannot be denied

But tell me friend, what stirs your soul?
What drives you toward your distant goal?
What do you work for, in quiet grace
That gives your life its noble place?

Shadows of a Titan

Upon my *father's* shoulder, firm and wide
I find the world's safest place to hide
No fear can pierce, no storm can break
For in his presence, the world I forsake

He is the strength that stirs my soul
A beacon bright that makes me whole
My role model, silent yet profound
In his quiet wisdom, I am found

He stands beside me, proud and true
No fear remains when he's in view
My courage, my guide, my constant friend
With him, I know I will transcend

Unyielding in love, unspoken, deep
He guards my spirit, guards my sleep
In him, a trust that cannot fail
A *father's love*, an endless tale

Beneath the Pen

Through *pain*, we are transformed and bent
Shaped by the force, the ache, the rent
Some wear their wounds like a bitter crown
Others lash out, as hearts break down

Some shout their grief to the world's cruel ear
While others retreat, consumed by fear
In silence, they carry the weight inside
A quiet burden, where tears collide

They say that pain, in the hands of art
Turns suffering's thread to a work of heart
Yet never do they whisper the truth unspoken
That art cannot heal the heart still broken

For *writers*, pain is a spark, a flame
But it leaves the soul never quite the same
Yes, the ink flows, but beneath the pen
The *hurt* lingers, and will, again and again